The Neighborhood of Suffering

David Widup

PUBLISHED BY ALSING RESERVOIR PRESS • ASHLAND, OREGON

Neighborhood of Suffering
by David Widup
© 2019 David Widup
Published by Alsing Reservoir Press, Ashland Oregon

Book design: booksavvystudio.com
Cover photo: Israelbest, courtesy of pixabay.com

ISBN: 978-1-7337365-0-3
First Edition
Printed in the United States of America

Dedicated to Cec,
my only safe place for so many years.

Contents

Close to Death

> If I am close to death and life support would
> only postpone the moment of my death:
>
> INITIAL ONE:
> ____ I want to receive tube feeding.
> ____ I want tube feeding only as my
> physician recommends.
> ____ DO NOT WANT tube feeding.

I don't know what it is to be close to death.
    Does that mean that it is nearby,
    and I can see it easily, without my glasses,
    or maybe it's not a space thing
    but a time thing and close to death means
    it could happen now,
    before punctuation gets put on the
    end of this line?

Or maybe, it is a course correction thing –
    close to death means I will die soon if I don't
    do something, like change course,
    veer hard left towards the center line,
    away from the ditch, sweat in my eyes
    another close call, one more.

I'm thinking there might be a death neighborhood,
    you know, across town,
    through the square with the nice shops,
    the Information Center stand with pamphlets
    the smiling old lady, the statue of the boy pissing
    in the fountain,
    past the park
    up on the hill.

Yes, that's where death is, up the hill,
   not down here in the suffering neighborhood
   by the railroad tracks and the wannabe parks
   built between the tracks and the hardware store,
   lumber yard and dog park and all the other places you
   never want to go, but have to
   from time to time,
   you know, for maintenance:
       change the light bulb,
          exercise the dog,
             fix the garage door.

What happens if someone thinks I'm close to death,
   you know, up the hill on the other side of the park,
   and I'm really just suffering and longing?
   Maybe I'm just at the hardware store being grumpy
   and silent because I hate to fix broken things,
   but I'm not close to dying, I feel OK, I'm just pissed
     because
   I'm doing stupid stuff. What happens if I'm
   doing maintenance and they think
   I'm close to death and pull the plug?
   The garage door doesn't get fixed,
   the light bulb stays burnt out and Nancy can't see
   when she walks downstairs for water in the middle
     of the night,
   Molly doesn't get her special dog treats and pouts
   when Mark comes and goes and can't give her something
   to let her know he loves her and will come back,
   take her outside and throw the ball when he gets here.
   What happens then?

Joe's Cup of Joe

It all started on a snowy night last February when Jim,
the guy that plows the streets around here
in Boothbay Harbor, Maine,
came around the corner too fast in his pickup truck
on his way, I am sure, to the Maintenance Yard on
     Main Street
just opposite Joe's Cup of Joe, where I am now sitting
drinking coffee with a grease stain floating on top,
grease I'm sure will clog my arteries and kill
     me some day,
just as dead as Jim is now,
buried up on the hill next to his Mom and Dad
and his son Jeremy, who bit the dust that same day,
but in a different place, up towards the dump,
two of them dead, buried the same day,
only Jim's wife left now, alone, working long hours
serving coffee and burgers at Joe's Cup of Joe,
watching the TV above the pass thru filled with plates,
the sound on mute, no
longer spending time with me.
     Imagine that.

Anniversary

47 years ago, today,
Custer threw imaginary rice,
Sonny tossed popcorn
that survived the prior
night's Kazoo Band
munchies.

Marie and I,
bride and groom,
freshly returned from our
destination wedding –
Kimball County courthouse
Nebraska, just miles
from the missile site
that was my home,
3 days on, 3 days off.

She was pregnant. I had
mono. We were broke.
Marriage was an answer
to a question that could
not quite form, an itch
no one could reach,
an unease that aroused
us, looking over each
other's' shoulder.

Get a Job

Bags of vermiculite,
soda ash or
cement mixer
one on top of another,
nine hours a day,
six days a week.
Sixty pounds per bag.

Dust everywhere,
under your fingernails,
mixed with sweat and, then -
a concrete factory
right there on
the end of your hand.

It dries and pulls the nail
away from your finger,
doesn't hurt much
at first. Then you see drops
of blood on your fingertips,
splatters on the factory floor.

Wipe it on your jeans,
pick up more dust for good measure,
lift a sixty-pound bag onto a pallet,
then another and another.
The nail separates more,
fingers outlined in blood.

The factory grinds,
dust fills the air, hoppers bang, pregnant
with powders dropped into sacks,
stitched shut with a whap, whap, whap.
They lie in waiting
for a pallet bed
crawling on the conveyor
belt, grinding away.

Wrap your fingers
in thin gauze tape,
put on a pair of latex gloves.
They tear with the next bag
thrown on the pallet.
Start over,
off with the latex gloves,
now in shreds,
off with the bloody gauze wrap
stuck on your fingers.

Your fingertip swells
like a bulb.
New latex gloves now,
and an old pair of canvas
gloves from the back.

They're stiff and it's
hard to grab the bags,
throw them on the pallet.
One bag every 20 seconds,
three each moment.
One gets past,

kick it off the belt.
Fingers throbbing,
back muscles sore,
you squeeze your hands
harder through stiff gloves,
lift the next bag off the belt,
slap it on the pallet.

You wipe sweat from your forehead
with the back of your forearm.
The foreman comes by,
says you're docked for the gloves
you're bleeding into.

Me

of course, it's about me,
it couldn't be otherwise
I don't even know me
but I damn sure don't
know anyone else.

Not mom whose face
blends into my sister's,
my wives',
my own.
I think of Mom's
steely black
silver coal dust
hair, a tangle of con-
fusion.
Confusing
even me.

Me. what is left
after all the crap hardens,
a thin shell
cracked, flaking, dust
on the floor. What is
left.

for gone,
     left to die
          naked
               scared, alone.

Numbers Song

Here are some real numbers,
true and accurate.
I attended 7 grade schools,
1 middle school,
3 high schools.
I was 18
when I landed in Bien Hoa,
almost 20
when I returned to Phan Rang.
I have 5 kids
with 3 women, plus
3 stepchildren. Somewhere
there are 9 grandkids.

I have lived, I think,
in 24 dwellings
in 11 states
and 6 countries.
I am not a gypsy
or a lost, wandering soul.
Mom died 50 years ago,
Dad 23 – he lived 27
years without her.
With luck, I'll double that.
How's your math
holding up?
Cec died the same year that
I put Ethel down, just 4
years ago. Grandma lived to
101 ½, most of it good time.

Honest, this wasn't my idea,
I don't even like numbers,
they have just done me in
over and over and over again.
I don't keep track, say
"Hey, this is my 25th dwelling
in my 12th state or
maybe 7th country."
I had to count them up
just now.
I wrote it all down once –
the dates, the places, the schools,
the deaths, the losses -
that was the last time
I almost had a drink.
What harm can 6 oz. of
13 proof Chardonnay do to my
AST and ALT scores?
Tell the truth,
I am.
How are your numbers?

Where I'm From

after George Ella Lyon

I am from a rollaway bed and plastic toy soldiers,
   from a bow and arrow of sticks and twigs.
I am from the back of the station wagon,
   light blue, split plastic seats, tobacco infused.
I am from the Sacred Gardens of Kyoto, quiet etched
   grounds, each step a whispered prayer -
   wandering alone, lost, hypnotized.

I am from a sweat stained, Epiphone fretboard and
   Winston cigarettes, from Runkle and Wilson
   and Peart blood.
I'm from drinking booze to numb the pain
   and tears of shame for what I have,
from *Don't lie to me!* and *We can't afford that.*
I'm from Evening Prayer, sung *a cappella*
   by children in a small stone chapel,
   "Let us Bless the Lord." "Thanks be to God."

I'm from Cec and Sherron and Uncle Skip and Aunt
   Margaret, from cinnamon toast for breakfast and
   pot roast on Sundays.
From the life my father tried to take, but failed,
my mother's - drowned in bourbon.

I have her torn leather notebook
   with yellowed pages, old and cracking,
   poems by others, notes of her own.
I am in her journal, it was kept for me -
   sadness on every page,
   hope between the lines.

Family Tree

Hemmingway wrapped wire
around the trigger, the other
end tied to his toe, put both
barrels in his mouth and
kicked his life away.
Drunk.

That first sweet sip,
the urge each day lying in bed,
a promise that lured me upright,
it has exacted its duty.

Uncle Skip went first, driving
to work drunk on Monday morning.
Then Mom married the bottle,
drowned in her vomit at 3 PM,
left Dad to figure it out.

Her parents, Clell and Mabel,
gave up after Mom's funeral.
Rocking back and forth on the old sofa,
eyes vacant, Grandma said,
"No parent should have to
bury all their children."
then moved on the next day.

My wife, finally sober, passed
in an Arizona halfway house,
asleep on the living room sofa,
alone, on the eve of the century.

A brother in a San Jose motel room,
gone at least a week when found,
dozens of empties on the floor,
under the bed, in his pockets.

My sister Cec, in the ICU,
finally sober, but wrecked,
tubes in her arms, out her groin,
lights too white, always on,
eyes begging for peace.

My oldest child passed out,
six-inch scalp gash, four hours
on a stairwell floor, blood
seeping, turning purple, then black.
"I can quit" he'd said that morning.

I don't know my family,
or even what a family is,
how to be a father, a husband.
The legacy of a tired life,
tied to the allure,
the cutting edge,
the numbing.

We live your dying
drunken torture
every day.

I Had No Idea

Mom died - it was the beginning
of my journey to Vietnam.
She died alone, in her bed
on a hot July afternoon in 1967,
the summer before my Senior year,
in a suburban New Jersey house
without air conditioning.
I was in an Indiana book bindery.
We were both sweating at 3:30 PM
when she let out her last breath.

She hated the war. She loved me.
If she had lived, I wouldn't have gone.
I ran away that summer,
I didn't think it would kill her.
I can't get the image of her
pale face with gray black hair
spilling onto the white pillow,
eyes barely shut, lips slightly apart
out of my mind.
I cannot separate my going
to Vietnam from her death.

I joined the Air Force. I had no idea
they would give me a gun,
send me to Vietnam within a year.

I had no idea that at 18, I'd be in charge
of a small armory and security for
400 men and $25 million of equipment.

I had no idea, that day Mom died
as I looked up at the clock
on the shipping dock wall.
No idea at all.

Black and White

My image of Nam
before I got there
was black and white,
what I had seen on a TV set.

I thought about the war
as good guys, victims all,
fighting a miserable, foreign war.
Once *Life* had black and white
pictures of the men killed
in Vietnam the prior week.

I can remember every hour
between when I got orders to go
and touchdown at Bien Hoa.
Two months left at Altus AFB,
one month of leave, home,
two months of jungle training.
I still remember dreams of Canada,
but never figured out how.
I never thought it would happen.
It seemed so unreal, those long
five months.
I kept thinking I would
wake up.

Fifty Years Ago, Today
(18 SEP 68)

Rainbow, rainbow don't be blue
four more years and you'll be through
Am I right or wrong?

5:00 AM.
My father wakes me up.
I smell he's showered and shaved,
wonder again how he
never seems to sleep.

There's grey light outside my window.
I hear the birds, a car every so often.
I get out of bed,
dead man rising from the grave.

He drives me to Newark,
the Armed Forces Induction Center.
We don't talk as we pass yellow
school buses with black lettering
moving to their first pick up.
High School kids at the foot of the hill,
smoking cigarettes, laughing.
I know nothing,
nothing at all.
I light another cigarette.

My father listens to classical music
as we drive Routh 46 East.
His uniform fits him well,

I wonder about the ribbons on his chest.
He is silent, retired eight years
now. I was prouder of him
when he wore a uniform every day.
I would never tell him that.

10:30 AM
My father swears me in.
We stand as a group, thirty or forty
young men in jeans and long hair
pledge to love, honor and obey.
Tired and confused, he looks at
me as he administers
the time-honored oath
to serve, honor, protect,
he looks at me
as if he's never seen me before.

1:00 PM
My father is in my thoughts,
his wet steel eyes still
staring at me being inducted,
as I get another physical,
strange men squeezing
my balls, putting their middle finger
up my asshole too far,
for too long.
I wonder if he knows
this is happening to his oldest son.

11:00 PM
My father is absent, again,
late that night, standing in
the spotlight with my squad -
79 new companions.
They are quiet now, shifting
from foot to foot. I'm sweating,
even though it's getting cold.
I hear him before I see
my Drill Sargent's black face
under a dark olive, Smokey the Bear hat,
above a facade of starched khakis:

"LISTEN UP MOTHERFUCKERS.
WHAT I'M ABOUT TO TELL YOU
MAY SAVE YOUR ASS!"

Short Timer

My squadron was unusual –
we went over together
were all short together –

> so short we needed a ladder to climb up onto a dime,
> so short we had to look up to look down,
> so short we couldn't start anything for fear of not
> being able to finish,
> need to take a crap, but don't want to miss my plane,
> want to smoke a cigarette, but don't want to waste it.

Short was less than 100 days left
in country. Short meant FIGMO.
Short timers had their own culture,
their own set of rules.
Some slept in bunkers,
afraid the first rocket in would catch them sleeping.
Many stopped booze and drugs.
Those that had started out fucking
worried about the clap and VD.
Everyone who was going to take R&R had.
There was nothing left looking forward
but home.

I was crazy

I was sure I was going to die.
I was stoned most of the time,
flew an airplane for kicks,
went up in a Huey gunship
in the middle of a rocket attack.
I was sure I was going to die.
I thought about extending
for another seven months,
but didn't.
I quit writing home.
I mostly hurt from head to toe –
afraid to stay and afraid to go.

Bien Hoa to Tokyo

i

We're all headed home, bags under our eyes as dark and
    almost as big as the duffels we dragged when we
    boarded, just as the sun came up.

Last night I slept on the ground. I dreamed I was flying
    above the base, arms outstretched

gliding on air, close enough to the ground to see the
    people walking, the planes on the runway,

trucks coming and going, guys lined up like a long snake,
    headed further in country. Soaring.

Soaring, that's what I was doing. Dreaming taught me to
    soar. Dreaming taught me the body is less than a
    dream.

ii

Jimmy Scarpatti and I sit together, an old 707, but at least
    it has real seats that recline and stewardesses -

the best-looking women I have seen in 366 days, that's
    for sure - to bring food and water. But they send out
    vibes to leave them alone. Whatever...

We've been together for a year and I don't know him.
    He's from Brooklyn, smiles a lot, drinks little, stays
    out of the way.

I don't sleep on airplanes, he says, before we take off. Just
    so you know. I'll just sit here and read and smoke.
    Maybe have a shot or two. You?

No, I don't sleep much on planes either. I don't have
    anything to do but get there. Along for the ride.

Jimmy's by the window, I'm on the aisle. How long's the
    flight I ask. Bien Hoa, Tokyo, Anchorage, McGuire.

Long time. Depends. Could be a day, maybe more.
    When will we get there? What day will it be?
    No clue.

Jimmy looks out the window as we turn onto the runway,
    I don't even know what day it is there now.

Rolling, nose up, wheels up. I wait for a blast or
    explosion. Still shaking and trying to hide it, chain
    smoking,

waiting for the end. Just the whoosh of the long jetliner
    aimed upward. Dodged another one, I think.

What're you going home to? Jimmy asks. My vision is
    closing in, my head started to throb when we took
    off. I'm off to Francis E. Warren next.

That's in Colorado, huh? Wyoming, I say. Wyoming. Shit.
    Is that a place? My mind is sore. I can't think of
    anything to say.

Jimmy says, I don't care about this, I'm getting out when we get back. I'm so short I need a ladder to climb up on a dime.

How much time you got left? I tell him two years. Two years? You're still green. Whistle britches. The stewardess comes on the PA:

no smoking in the aisles or bathroom, only drink what we give you, water, coffee

soda pop, we'll confiscate any open hooch that you brought on board, no food in flight,

in Tokyo and Anchorage you can buy food, the stewardesses have the last word,

any violation of these rules and you will be detained at the next stop and returned to Bien Hoa

handed over to the Military Police for processing. Welcome home. Thank you for your service.

What are you going back to Jimmy? My father wants me to join the family business, he says. The plane banks hard and I see the ocean out the window.

The jet engines speed and shriek, my hand starts to shake. I'm confused, haven't felt anything in some time.

I get up to go to the latrine after we level off. The PA
   barks *No smoking in the aisle way!* I sit down again.

Jimmy chuckles. Imagine that, we wander around the
   jungle for a year building towers and runways out of
   nothing, trying not to get killed

by teenagers with submachine guns, have our wives and
   girlfriends dump us and now we're being talked to
   like we're in first grade.

Butt in the ashtray, I head back to the latrine.

Coming Home

I came home but didn't get out.
When I landed at Ft. Dix that muggy
September night in 1970,
I had two years left.
Depositing two cigarette packs
full of "The World's Best Grass"
in the Amnesty Box,
I took off my jungle fatigues,
put them in the trash can,
put on civilian clothes.
I was clean and sober,
felt hungover and numb.
It was a black night,
thunderstorms without lightening.

I dozed in someone's car
all the way to my sister's
in New York City, still dark, wet.
I just sat and looked at them.
I didn't know what to say.
They seemed strange to me.
I felt their anticipation
with every breath.
I don't remember what was said,
though we talked until dawn.

In a laundromat that week,
I remember being ashamed,
how stunning,
beautiful, the women were.
I remember being
dirty, unworthy.
They looked at me,
question marks, scorn.

Coming home was hard.
Still is.

Rock Lake

One mile
across, one mile back.
At first, I kept looking up
to see the landmarks -
the boathouse over, my house back.
Later, I just swam, the warm water
caressing me, my arms,
my chest, between my legs.

My sister and I sat in the water
on hot, humid Florida afternoons.
The water to our waists,
we talked and sat and looked.
I was scared, she was lonely,
until the tables turned.

Up the sandy lakeshore,
across the maidencane and knotweed,
surrounded by crabgrass
our red clay patio held white
wrought iron table and chairs,
Mom sat there smoking, sipping
bourbon and sweating. Waiting
to explode.

In the ICU

My sister lays in a bed,
large hose down her throat,
mouth held open with a large plastic "O,"
her arms an octopus
of needled tubes.
Monitors on metal arms
flash numbers and lines,
humming, beeping
through the glare.

Her eyes are mostly closed,
vacant when open,
tear from time to time,
plead *Let me go.*
A selfish request, this,
but how can I say "No?"
How can I say "Yes?"
Her gaze goes into a
blank space, out of the ICU.

What is most intense
is the light,
bright white light,
always on.
There is no night or day,
dusk and dawn are gone.
The ICU
is a luminary assault,
a never-ending day.

I think of her garden at home,
green and rocky and wild,
the smell of dried grasses
and summer wildflowers
in my nose, earthen air
around me, in me.
This is her ashes' home.
Not in the ICU that's
bright, even in the darkness.

Fragments Found Inside My Sister

after Nick Flynn

_i_

On the side of the road
    in my pink dress, waiting

To be saved, by someone, anyone.
    A young sailor stopped and smiled,

helped Dad fix the flat, took a $5 bill
    winked and hopped into his truck.

_ii_

Invisible, that's what I was. Without form, I
    pushed a finger through myself.

I swam across Rock Lake and back,
    two miles, but only for myself.

Wanting to stop and rest, I swam on,
    wanting to ride the crest home.

iii

Those kids, like chicks with open mouths,
    Never full, there was not enough

Food, love, money, truth, stuff, stuff -
    a cacophony now, my ears hurt.

I took care of them, made it right
    held them dear in the cold, cold night.

_iv_

Indiana farm houses were the best,
  we laid in bed and kissed and slept.

Her touch was electricity. Shot from crown
  to groin. Summer breezes scant reprieve.

Opening my eyes was hard, hard
  taking in her long hair and painted eyes.

_v_

I just wanted to be a girl
  and to be loved.

I tasted lemon juice and honey
  only together, never apart.

My homes were frail, quaking, vacant
  like peace or Mom.

_vi_

My throat hurts. I cannot sleep.
  I am worn smooth and soft.

I chose this life and now
  it's time to go.

I'm tired,
  let me go.

Time

Later,
much later,
we decided
when
and how
to end
her life.
I'm not
over it, yet.
Time has a way...

I smell the soft perfume she used to wear,
back when she still cared. It's like
she's still here. I hope
I'm not holding her back.
Time has a way...

This peach has such a thin skin, it tears
with a light touch, and under
is that sweet, wet fruit, the good
stuff. It's on my
fingers, face, forearms,
moving, covering. This seed,
hard, sharp, bitter,
the source of all.

Time.
It has this way of caving in
on itself, a nuclear implosion.

Memories.

Holding the pick-up-sticks in my fist,
opening fingers, sticks splay
with a clatter.
Events jumble -
was it the blue or red
stick that moved last time?

Last to Know

GEICO just called,
Mark hit a pedestrian with the truck
either yesterday or three weeks ago,
they're not sure.
News to me.

My sister called,
Mom died,
not sure at home or where,
last night or maybe this morning,
had been sick for weeks.
News to me.

Sherron called,
my sister was in ICU,
cardiac arrest from complications,
maybe the heart or could be the liver,
just had surgery at Columbia Presbyterian.

Orders home came in,
going to Wyoming
or maybe its Colorado
doesn't matter, out West
away from my family.
News to me.

I'm the last to know
because there is nothing worth knowing
or maybe I'm not worth telling
or maybe the news just doesn't matter,
although I wonder if Mark hurt
the pedestrian,
I'm not sure.

Nowhere

I live in the middle of nowhere. Actually, it is not
    nowhere, it's no-where, as in not near anyplace
    people tend to go,

unless they are lost and looking for somewhere to get
    found. But then, when they get here, they think

they are close to where they need to be, because when
    they are here they are not nowhere, they are here

and that is better than not being anywhere, I'm thinking.
    The hills outside my windows are green all year,
    that's a blessing—

to be able to see life even in the dead of winter when
    most things are. The bears are sleeping,

the leaves have fallen off the trees, the flowers are dead
    stalks in a hard, cold soil that won't give up

anything, anywhere. I put my head in the pine covered
    hills to sleep and lift it out in the morning.

The smell is sandalwood musk. Green. My daughter says
    that this place is idyllic, magical, mystical, almost
    perfect.

The soft verdant hillside, the silence at night and all the
    people that aren't here, but are there,
    wherever that is.

What more could you ask for? - her question that
    hangs in the air.

Songs

Ready to rock and roll
with Kahuna 3.0
All the way down town, man
downtown, all the way
down. Go down, fall
through the floor, fall
through the ceiling, fall
through the walls, rock bottom,
downtown, down to the pound.

Now, let's be clear,
there is honesty being spoken now—
real and, therefore, true.
It can't be false or made up,
where would it come from,
thin air? gasses and fumes? spirits?
It didn't just end up in my head,
magically one moment.
The monsters with legs of eels
and flashing red eyes,
those did not just get deposited
in the checking account of my soul,
a surprise wire transfer
from God.
I don't think so.
The monsters are real,
they cannot be imaginary.
No more pretending.

OK, so some things
are a little muddled,
not to the letter of the law.
Forgive me judge,
I have exaggerated.
But even an exaggeration
cannot be all made up.
I am not exalting vapor,
I am yelling reality
so that it can be seen,
clearly, like the bottom of a sparkling
sunlit shallow swimming pool,
the water in the pool magnifies
the beauty of the blue stones below,
like my soul magnifies God's glory.
It's not make believe, it's like sperm
invading the wall of an egg under a
microscope—it's real even though
it's not apparent. It's not make believe.
There, if you still doubt me, Santa
brings presents for Christmas,
the Tooth Fairy puts quarters
under pillows, the stork delivers
babies and Jesus is in love,
maybe in love with you,
right now,
today, here.
Jesus loves you.

Some songs are blast real—
under an examination light without
grace. Some, I'm not sure which,

maybe not so stark real, but
in the vicinity.
Maybe not in the same Zip code, but
definitely, definitely in the same
area code. One SMSA for real songs
and almost real songs. Some songs,
maybe more, are the right notes,
just the order has changed –
same key, different tune.
Kind of like singing "Get Back"
to the tune of "Gimme Shelter."
Others, well maybe I got the key
wrong. I'm not perfect –
that's the truth.
C Major and G Major are close,
that's easy to fake and it's still real.
E Minor – now that's a
big exaggeration. I mean
if it is a G Major poem
we're talking commanding,
bright highs and solid mid-range,
a statement – I am here
you hear? Got it, dude?
E Minor is a requiem in
a song, bury me, throw the
dirt on top, say a prayer, move on.
Once E Minor comes to town,
hide the children, pay the bills
and get ready to die, damn it.

So, here's the issue – I'm not
entirely sure what is true
and what is in the same
area code and what is a small
change in notes within a key,
what is a change in key and
what is a new tune with
altered lyrics all together.
I mean I think I know it,
but only after it is sung,
and even then, I'm not so sure –
anyway, it is not deception, that's
what I'm trying to say –
it's not deception, it's confusion,
exhaustion, limbs like weights,
heart fallen deep into my belly,
I just get confused when I'm tired
and I'm exhausted now to where
I just need to sit a few,
maybe get a cup, maybe rest my eyes
but only for a second or two.
I promise

David Widup lives in Ashland, Oregon. He is a poet, coach and editor who has previously authored two books of poetry and several chapbooks. David's poetry has also appeared in various literary journals including *ACM*, *Rattle*, *ONTHEBUS* and *ZZYVA*. He holds an MFA in Creative Writing program from Pacific University.

www.ingramcontent.com/pod-product-compliance
Lightning Source LLC
Chambersburg PA
CBHW061200040426
42445CB00013B/1754